Pebble® Plus

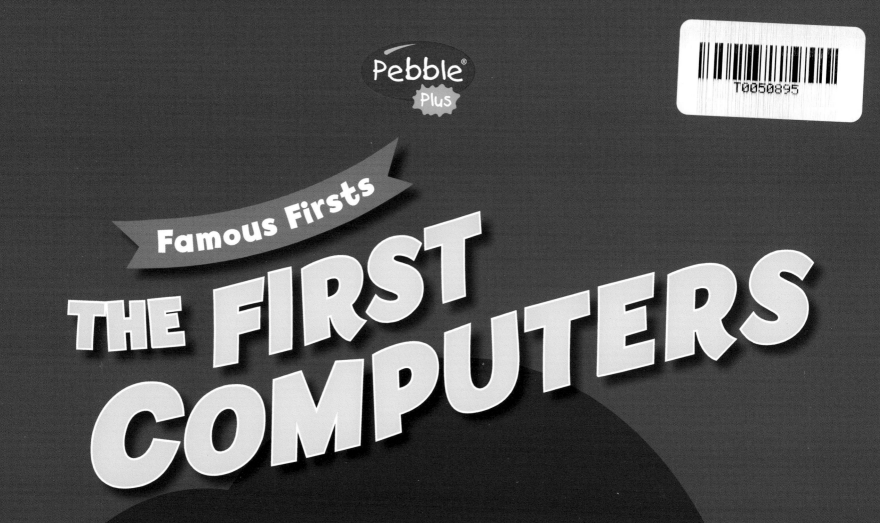

Famous Firsts

THE FIRST COMPUTERS

by Megan Cooley Peterson

Consulting Editor: Gail Saunders-Smith, PhD

Consultant: Jonson Miller, PhD
Associate Teaching Professor of History and Science,
Technology, and Society
Drexel University

CAPSTONE PRESS
a capstone imprint

Pebble Plus is published by Capstone Press,
1710 Roe Crest Drive, North Mankato, Minnesota 56003
www.capstonepub.com

Library of Congress Cataloging-in-Publication Data
Peterson, Megan Cooley, author.
  The first computers / Megan Cooley Peterson.
     pages cm.—(Famous firsts)
  Summary: "Large photographs and simple text describe eight early computers"—Provided by publisher.
  Includes bibliographical references and index.
  ISBN 978-1-4914-0575-8 (hb)— ISBN 978-1-4914-0643-4 (pb)—ISBN 978-1-4914-0609-0 (eb)
1. Computers—Juvenile literature. 2. Computers--History—Juvenile literature. I. Title.
  QA76.23.P475 2015
  004—dc23   2014001805

Editorial Credits
Erika L. Shores, editor; Terri Poburka, designer; Svetlana Zhurkin, media researcher; Laura Manthe, production specialist

Photo Credits
AP Images: Frederick News-Post, 7; Getty Images: Bettmann, cover, 19, Bletchley Park Trust, 9, Historical, 11; Newscom: ITAR-TASS/Alexandra Mudrats, 17, Zumapress/Robin Nelson, 15; Shutterstock: Monkey Business Images, 5; Wikipedia: Bcos47, 21, Jitze Couperus, 13

Note to Parents and Teachers

The Famous Firsts set supports national social studies standards related to science, technology, and society. This book describes and illustrates the first computers. The images support early readers in understanding the text. The repetition of words and phrases helps early readers learn new words. This book also introduces early readers to subject-specific vocabulary words, which are defined in the Glossary section. Early readers may need assistance to read some words and to use the Table of Contents, Glossary, Read More, Internet Sites, Critical Thinking Using the Common Core, and Index sections of the book.

Table of Contents

The First Computers

Computers are everywhere.
These machines help us
find information and solve
problems. Discover some
of the first computers.

Electronic Computers

Early computers were made
to solve math problems.
The ABC solved 29 problems
at once. It was also the first
computer run by electricity.

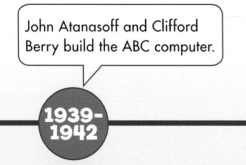

John Atanasoff and Clifford
Berry build the ABC computer.

1939-1942

Breaking Codes

British engineers built the Colossus.

This computer could break

secret codes. It broke thousands

of codes during World War II

(1939–1945).

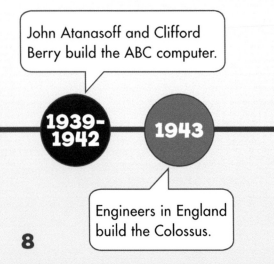

John Atanasoff and Clifford
Berry build the ABC computer.

1939–1942

1943

Engineers in England
build the Colossus.

9

Gaining Speed

The ENIAC computer solved thousands of math problems per second. This computer weighed 30 tons (27 metric tons). It filled an entire room!

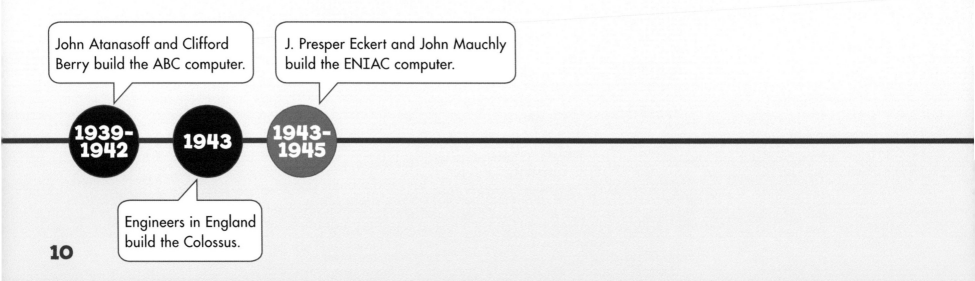

John Atanasoff and Clifford Berry build the ABC computer.

J. Presper Eckert and John Mauchly build the ENIAC computer.

1939–1942

1943

1943–1945

Engineers in England build the Colossus.

Workers had to plug and unplug cables on ENIAC.

Supercomputers

The CDC 6600 could do

3 million tasks per second.

It was the first computer

to be called a "supercomputer."

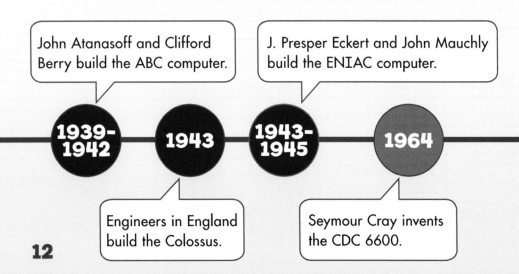

John Atanasoff and Clifford Berry build the ABC computer.

J. Presper Eckert and John Mauchly build the ENIAC computer.

1939–1942

1943

1943–1945

1964

Engineers in England build the Colossus.

Seymour Cray invents the CDC 6600.

Personal Computers

The first personal computers came in kits. Customers put them together. The Altair 8800 was a popular kit. Switches on the front ran the computer.

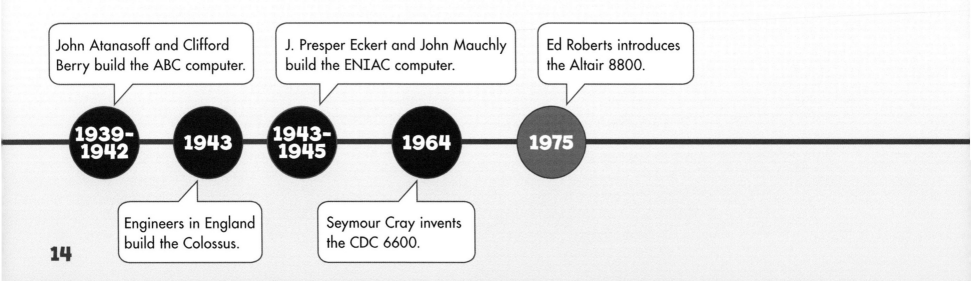

John Atanasoff and Clifford Berry build the ABC computer.

J. Presper Eckert and John Mauchly build the ENIAC computer.

Ed Roberts introduces the Altair 8800.

1939–1942 **1943** **1943–1945** **1964** **1975**

Engineers in England build the Colossus.

Seymour Cray invents the CDC 6600.

Steve Jobs and Steve Wozniak built the Apple II. This early personal computer had a color display. Many schools used the Apple II.

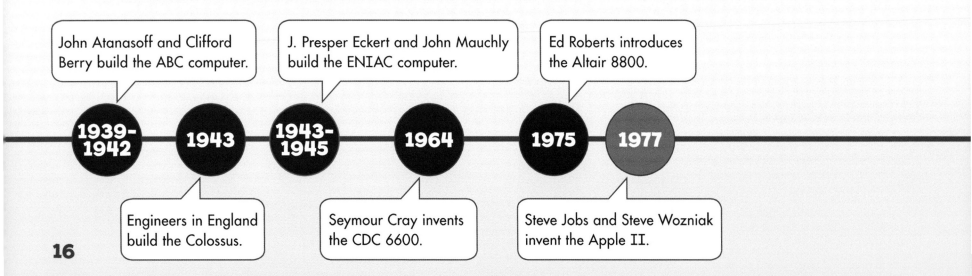

John Atanasoff and Clifford Berry build the ABC computer.

J. Presper Eckert and John Mauchly build the ENIAC computer.

Ed Roberts introduces the Altair 8800.

1939-1942 **1943** **1943-1945** **1964** **1975** **1977**

Engineers in England build the Colossus.

Seymour Cray invents the CDC 6600.

Steve Jobs and Steve Wozniak invent the Apple II.

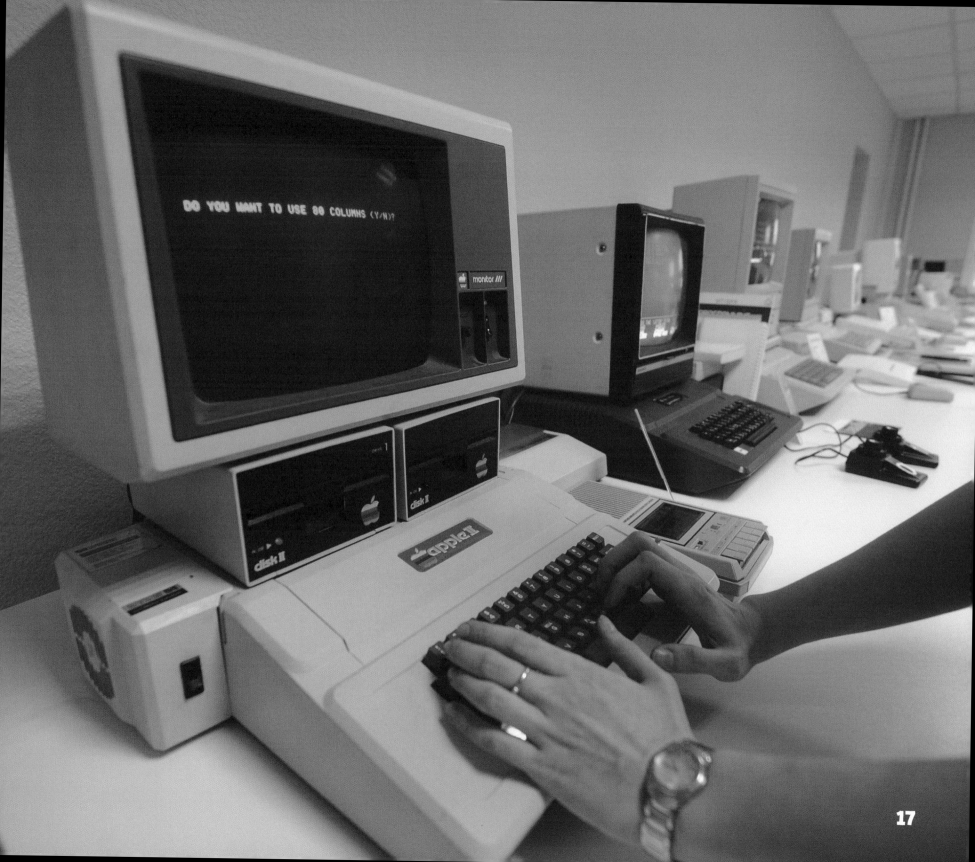

Laptops

People wanted to travel with their computers. The Osborne 1 fit under an airplane seat. This early laptop weighed 24 pounds (11 kilograms).

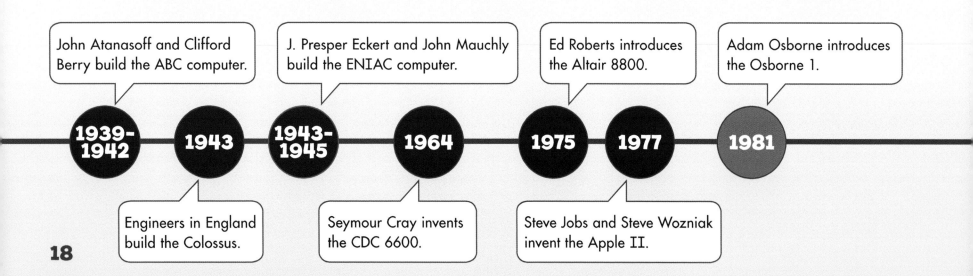

John Atanasoff and Clifford Berry build the ABC computer.

J. Presper Eckert and John Mauchly build the ENIAC computer.

Ed Roberts introduces the Altair 8800.

Adam Osborne introduces the Osborne 1.

1939-1942

1943

1943-1945

1964

1975

1977

1981

Engineers in England build the Colossus.

Seymour Cray invents the CDC 6600.

Steve Jobs and Steve Wozniak invent the Apple II.

Smartphones

Ring, ring! The Simon was

a computer and a cell phone.

It was the first smartphone.

Today many people

use smartphones.

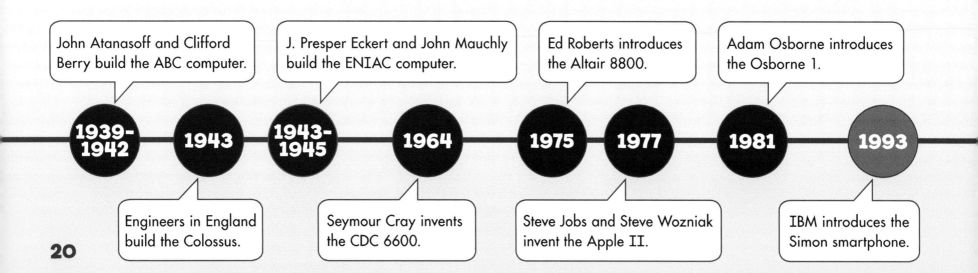

John Atanasoff and Clifford Berry build the ABC computer.

J. Presper Eckert and John Mauchly build the ENIAC computer.

Ed Roberts introduces the Altair 8800.

Adam Osborne introduces the Osborne 1.

1939-1942   1943   1943-1945   1964   1975   1977   1981   1993

Engineers in England build the Colossus.

Seymour Cray invents the CDC 6600.

Steve Jobs and Steve Wozniak invent the Apple II.

IBM introduces the Simon smartphone.

Glossary

code—a system of letters, symbols, and numbers used to send secret messages

electricity—a natural force that can be used to make light and heat or to make machines work

engineer—a person who uses science and math to plan, design, or build

secret—information known only to oneself or a few people

supercomputer—the fastest and most powerful computer available

Read More

Gould, Jane. *Steve Jobs.* Jr. Graphic American Inventors. New York: PowerKids Press, 2013.

Guillain, Charlotte. *Computers.* Jobs if You Like. Chicago: Heinemann Library, 2013.

Lee, Sally. *Staying Safe Online.* Staying Safe. Mankato, Minn.: Capstone Press, 2012.

Internet Sites

FactHound offers a safe, fun way to find Internet sites related to this book. All of the sites on FactHound have been researched by our staff.

Here's all you do:

Visit *www.facthound.com*

Type in this code: 9781491405758

 Super-cool stuff! Check out projects, games and lots more at **www.capstonekids.com**

Critical Thinking Using the Common Core

1. What were some of the reasons people invented computers? (Integration of Knowledge and Ideas)

2. Why was the CDC 6600 called a supercomputer? (Key Ideas and Details)

Index